Cross and Crescent:

The Story of the Crusades

CROSS and CRESCENT:

 The Story of the Crusades

by Richard Suskind

illustrated by Victor Lazzaro

W· W· NORTON & COMPANY· INC· NEW YORK

For *Marc Robert Lopez*

Contents

Venice

Const

Byzantine Empire

SICILY

Mediterran

CRETE

Black Sea

Seljuk Turks

Edessa

...ople

Aleppo

Antioch

RHODES

CYPRUS

Beirut

Acre

Sea

Jaffa

KINGDOM OF JERUSALEM

JERUSALEM

Alexandria

Cairo

Why the Crusades Began

FOR MANY HUNDREDS OF YEARS BEFORE THE FIRST CRUSADE, DEVOUT Christians from all over Europe made pilgrimages to the Holy Land. They went there to worship at the shrines in Jerusalem, Nazareth, Bethlehem, and the other places that had played important parts in the life of Jesus.

These voyages were very long and hard and dangerous even in times of peace. French or English pilgrims, for example, had to travel more than two thousand miles each way, over mountains and across deserts, in the heat of summer and the cold and storms of winter. They had to protect themselves against robbers on land and pirates at sea, and for food and shelter they had to depend on the kindness and good will of the people whose countries they crossed.

The first part of the journey was usually fairly safe, for it was through lands whose inhabitants had the same religion as the pilgrims. They were members of the Church of Rome — what we call Roman Catholic today — and accepted the Pope as spiritual leader. In these lands the pilgrims often passed the night in one of the many monasteries, and were fed and sheltered by the monks.

Farther along the route to the Holy Land, in what is now Greece or Yugoslavia, the pilgrims entered the Byzantine Empire.

1

This great empire, which played an important part in several of the Crusades, included most of the countries bordering the eastern end of the Mediterranean Sea. Until the middle of the eleventh century, the Byzantines had belonged to the Church of Rome also. But then they broke away and formed the Orthodox Eastern Church. They used Greek instead of Latin in their services and did not accept the Pope as spiritual leader. Nevertheless they usually treated the pilgrims with kindness and respect.

Then, after weeks of slow, difficult travel by land and sea, the pilgrims left the last Christian outpost behind and entered territory that was ruled by Mohammedans. This was the most dangerous part of the journey, for in the Middle Ages — the period of history with which this book is concerned — Christians and Mohammedans were usually at war with each other.

Islam, or Mohammedanism, was the last of the world's great religions to develop. After the death of its founder, the prophet Mohammed, in A.D. 632, his followers raised the banner of Islam (emblazoned with a crescent to indicate that Mohammedanism, like the crescent moon, was waxing in size and power) and conquered a vast empire extending from India in the east to Spain in the west.

Most of the inhabitants of these lands adopted the religion of their conquerors, so Mohammedans were of many races and colors. The Christians, however, called them all by one name: Saracens.

An important part of Mohammedanism is the *Hajj*. This is the pilgrimage that every Mohammedan is supposed to make to Mecca, the Arabian city in which Mohammed was born. Since the pilgrimage was so important in their own religion, the Mohammedan rulers of the Holy Land understood its importance to the Christians. For a long time they allowed groups of these visitors to enter the country, worship at the shrines, and leave in peace.

2

But Mohammedanism, like Christianity, has more than one branch, and in the eleventh century a fanatic, intolerant sect of the religion took control of the Holy Land. The members of this sect destroyed or desecrated several of the Christian shrines, including the most important one, The Church of the Holy Sepulcher. They attacked bands of pilgrims, killing some and selling the others into slavery. They made it impossible for pilgrims to enter the country.

At about the same time that this was happening in the Holy Land, other Saracens were attacking the Byzantine Empire. They defeated the Byzantine army in an important battle, conquered large areas of Asia Minor, and were generally so successful that the Byzantine Emperor sent a message to the Pope asking for help.

These were two of the reasons why, in November, 1095, the Pope preached a Crusade, or Holy War, against the Saracens and urged the kings and nobles of Western Europe to raise armies to conquer the Holy Land for Christendom. There was, however, another and even more important reason for the Pope's action. This had to do with the restless, warlike spirit of Europeans, a spirit that had been growing in intensity for several centuries and was now seeking an outlet. By proclaiming a Crusade, the Pope not only directed this spirit outward, against the Saracens, but also increased the power and influence of the Church. Since he was the head of the Church, his own personal power was increased as well.

TAKING THE CROSS

Europeans responded with great enthusiasm to the Pope's appeal. Almost every important noble in France, as well as many in Germany, England, Italy, Scandinavia, and the low countries, "took the Cross" — that is, wore a large cross of red cloth sewed to his surcoat, or outer garment, as evidence of his vow to take part in the Crusade — and set about raising and equipping his army for the

3

long march to the East. The motto of these Christian armies, said the Pope, should be *"Deus Vult!"* — *"*God Wills It!*"*

Why were so many men willing, even eager, to travel thousands of miles to fight an enemy they had never seen and knew almost nothing about? To help us answer this question, we should know something about the way people lived and thought in those days.

THE FEUDAL SYSTEM

During the Middle Ages, Europeans lived under a form of social organization called feudalism, or the feudal system, which regulated the lives of the three main social groups, or classes. These classes were: nobles, "men who fought"; peasants, "men who labored"; and clergy, "men who prayed." Laws and customs of feudalism developed gradually, beginning with the fall of the Roman Empire and continuing throughout the reign of Emperor Charlemagne. They reached their full development after Charlemagne died and his empire was broken up by invading Vikings from the north, Magyars from the east, and Saracens from Spain and North Africa. These laws and customs varied somewhat from country to country, but in general they provided a system in which the weak and defenseless were protected by the strong, and in which they paid for this protection by performing various duties and services.

Each country was divided into many domains or estates, some of them very large, which were ruled by barons who were often richer and more powerful than the king himself. In theory, all land belonged to the king and these barons were his tenants-in-chief. In practice, because roads and communications were so poor, the barons were independent rulers. They maintained or increased their power by giving "fiefs" — that is, castles with a few square miles of land

A feudal manor

surrounding them — to knights. In return, the knights swore to be faithful to the baron, to defend him against his enemies, and to supply him with a certain number of armed, mounted men for a certain number of days of military service every year. The usual period of military service was forty days, from which we get "quarantine," the French word for forty. The size and value of the fief determined the exact number of men the knight agreed to supply. Before a knight was "invested" with his fief, there was a formal ceremony in which he gave "homage" to the baron and became his "vassal."

A knight's training

THE MEN WHO FOUGHT

The noble's main business in life was fighting, and he began preparing for it at a very early age. When he was seven years old, he was taken from his parents and put into another noble household to be trained as a knight. There he toughened his body with gradually harder exercises and tests of endurance. He spent hours every day practicing with the sword and the shield, riding or "tilting" at the "quintain" — a barrel or a sack suspended from a pole — with the lance, swinging the two-handed battle-ax, the spike-studded mace, and fighting mock battles with his instructors and fellow students. He learned to ride the powerful great horse, which carried the heavily armored knights into battle, and the smaller, faster animals that were used for hunting. He learned how to "man," or handle

7

the various types of falcon, the peregrine, the merlin, the gyrfalcon, that were used for hunting birds and other small game, and how packs of hounds were used to hunt deer, wild boar, rabbits, and,

Knights hunting

occasionally, bear. From the women of the household, he learned table manners, how to dance, and how to speak elegantly and turn a courtly phrase.

Sometime between the ages of eighteen and twenty-two, the young noble was "dubbed" a knight. During the reign of Emperor Charlemagne (A.D. 768-814), this was a simple ceremony in which the knight-to-be was given a sharp blow on the chest or side of the neck — "the only blow that a knight must not return" — and handed his sword and spurs. In the later Middle Ages, however, it was much more elaborate. It began the night before the ceremony,

when the young noble stood a "vigil" at the altar, then bathed and went to sleep in an immaculate bed. In the morning he was dressed in a robe of white linen or silk, which symbolized purity. Over this he put on a scarlet robe, symbolic of the blood he must be ready to spill in defense of the Church. He wore brown boots to remind him that man is of the earth and must return there, and a white belt, symbolic, again, of purity. Then he heard a solemn mass, was given

9

the "accolade" by a bishop, that is, touched on the right shoulder with the flat of his sword, and handed his spurs by a layman. From that moment on he was a knight, bound by the code of chivalry to

Single combat with blunted lances

10

defend the weak against the strong and the poor against the rich.

As an adult, the noble hunted, fought and jousted at tournaments. Much of Europe was still covered with forests in which wild

animals abounded. When the noble was at home hardly a day went by that he did not hunt, for he had a household full of relatives and attendants to feed, and game was their chief source of meat. Day after day, winter and summer, the household was awakened by the blare of the huntsman's horn and his cry, "Up, seigneurs! We go to the forest!" When they returned from the hunt, the nobles washed and rested while the meat was cooked. They had prodigious appetites. The usual work-day meal consisted of six or seven courses of meat and fish, followed by bowls of fruit and nuts. It was all washed down with large amounts of wine, cider, and a fermented pear juice called perry.

Several times a year the noble took part in tournaments. These began as simple dress-rehearsals for combat in which teams of knights fought one another in what were called "mêlées." There were no rules, and men were often killed or badly hurt. Later on, tournaments became more elaborate, complicated rules were drawn up, and single-combats, or "jousts," became more popular than mêlées. So that fewer men would be injured, the knights fought with blunted lances and swords, and wore special, extra-heavy armor.

Apart from the hunt and tournaments, the noble spent a good deal of time at war. If he was not serving in the army of his baron or king, he was usually involved in a blood feud with one or more of his neighbors. The Pope tried, with little success, to control these blood feuds by declaring a "Truce of God," which forbade the fighting of private wars between Wednesday night and the following Monday morning of every week. One of the benefits of the Crusades was that, by giving the nobles a common enemy, they reduced the number of private wars. The chief sufferers in these blood feuds, however, were not the nobles but the peasants. Their cottages were burned to the ground, their crops destroyed, and their

12

sheep and cattle taken as booty. They themselves were sometimes killed and their wives and children scattered about the countryside.

THE MEN WHO LABORED

At any time and in any place, life has always been easier and more pleasant for a rich man than for a poor one. This was especially true in the Middle Ages, when there was a vast gulf between the way a noble and a peasant lived.

To begin with, almost none of the peasants were free men. The great majority of them were "serfs," that is, bound to the land they tilled, possessions of the lord who owned it. It was commonly said of a peasant that he "owned nothing but his belly," and in actual fact he was not much better off than if he had been a slave. Indeed, if a lord decided to sell a plot of land that was cultivated by a particular peasant, he could and usually did sell the peasant and his family with it. Entire villages sometimes changed hands in this manner.

Life in a medieval village must have been very hard and uncomfortable. The peasants' houses, one- or two-room wooden shacks with thatched roofs and earth floors, lined both sides of an unpaved street that was dusty in the summer and muddy in the winter. A house was sparsely furnished with a table and a couple of rough wooden stools, a few sacks filled with hay or straw that served as beds, and a couple of clay pots. There was no chimney, so the smoke from the fireplace, usually a scooped out hollow in the middle of the floor, had to find its way out through the small, glassless windows.

Peasants wore coarse woolen clothing the year round, rarely either washing or changing it. Their diet was simple, consisting mostly of flour boiled or baked with peas and beans, and with an occasional bit of fat thrown in for flavor. They had a small variety of cultivated fruits such as apples, pears, wild berries, and nuts in season, and a couple of vegetables. They ate very little meat. They were not permitted to hunt game, for the forests were reserved for nobles. The few sheep, cattle, and razorback pigs that they slaughtered every November and either salted down in barrels or dried, were scrawny, miserable creatures with not much flesh on their bones. Since tallow candles and oil-lamps were too expensive for anyone but the nobles and wealthier churchmen, the peasants rose with the sun and went to bed when it got dark.

In return for being allowed to farm an acre or two for himself and his family, the peasant had to farm the lord's land also. This work usually required three or four days a week during the spring and summer, and perhaps two days a week during the rest of the year. At harvest time, he had to bring in the lord's crops first, even if it rained and his own wheat and hay began to rot. The peasant had

A medieval village

to use the lord's mill to grind his flour and the lord's ovens to bake his bread, and he was required to pay for these services. He could not marry unless the lord approved of his bride. He could not move from one village to another. In addition to these burdens, and to the man-made disasters of the blood feud and the raiding of the "robber baron" from which he suffered, the peasant had to contend with natural disasters like floods, famine, drought, and disease.

There were only two ways in which a peasant youth could hope to "rise beyond his class." If he was strong and quick and brave, he could become a pikeman or crossbowman in the lord's service. Then, if the lord was successful in his campaigns, the peasant youth could sometimes accumulate enough booty to buy a farm, which he would then hold in "alod," that is, as a free man rather than a serf; or he might find favor with his lord and be appointed chief huntsman or falconer and in time be granted a small fief of his own.

The second way in which a peasant youth could rise beyond his class was by becoming a priest or a monk.

THE MEN WHO PRAYED

Life in the Middle Ages was as short as it was hard. Men died through violence, sometimes from trivial wounds that became infected. They died of starvation in the famines that occurred very often in the early summer, when the previous year's crops had been eaten and the new ones were not yet ready for harvesting. They died in the floods that periodically inundated large areas of France, Italy, and Germany. And, most frequently of all, they died of a variety of diseases that we have since learned to prevent and cure. Epidemics occurred regularly, some of them of extraordinary virulence. In the fourteenth century, for example, there was an epidemic of plague — the "Black Death" — that killed about three-fourths of

15

the entire population of Europe and Asia in less than twenty years.

Partly because death in all these forms was so common, religion played a very important part in the daily life of the people. It was natural for them to regard this life as a time of misery that had to be endured before they could enjoy the life-after-death as it was described by the Church. It was natural for them to think of God as close at hand, seeing and judging everyone and everything. And it was natural for them to regard monks and priests with special reverence, for it was believed that they were God's representatives on earth and that their prayers could assure one of going to heaven. Indeed, it would be hard to exaggerate the importance of religion in the Middle Ages. Everyone, no matter what his class, lived in dread of eternal damnation. Heaven and hell were very real places to them; and the state of their souls, which they examined constantly, was more important to them than the state of their bodies. Making a pilgrimage or going on Crusade was one way of doing penance, of atoning for past sins and of building credit in the eyes of God, and this was an important reason for the enthusiastic response to the Pope's preaching. Another reason was simply the European's love of fighting and his desire for booty and territory.

With the exception of the kings and a few nobles, the only men who could read and write were priests and monks. Without their chronicles, we would know very little about the history of the Middle Ages; and we would not have those magnificent illuminated manuscripts that are among the glories of this period. Most of the clergy knew at least two languages, their native tongue and Latin, and were thus able to communicate with one another regardless of where they were born and lived. Because they were so much better educated than most men, they were often employed as advisers and special envoys by barons and kings.

A monk transcribes a manuscript

The lower ranks of the clergy, the ordinary priests and monks, were filled from the peasant class. If a peasant youth was especially intelligent and devout and hard working, he could rise to the post of bishop, or abbot, or cardinal, or even, in rare cases, of Pope. These were the exceptions, however, and generally these important positions were filled by sons of the nobility.

By the law of primogeniture, which in Latin means "first-born," the eldest sons of a noble inherited all of his father's property. This prevented the great estates from being broken up when the noble died. But this also meant that the noble's other sons had no land except that which their older brother was kind enough to give them. It became customary for at least one of these younger sons to join the clergy, and these were the men who usually rose to positions of prominence in the Church.

At the time of the First Crusade, most of the monasteries scattered about Europe followed the rules laid down by Saint Benedict of Nursia, who died in A.D. 550. The "black monks," as the Benedictines were called because of the black robes they wore, lived hard, monotonous, closely regulated lives. Their day began at midnight with the service of matins, and ended with the service of compline at seven o'clock the next evening. The hours between were filled with work, study, and prayer. As time went on, other monastic orders were founded: Cluniac, Cistercian, Capuchin, Franciscan,

17

and many others. At their best, the monks in these monasteries were devout, scholarly men who had chosen this hard way of life in order to serve God and their fellow men. Unfortunately, as the monasteries grew rich through gifts of land and money, some of them became corrupt, slackly administered, filled with lazy, greedy monks who preyed upon the neighboring villages. There were pe-

A medieval monastery

riodic attempts to remedy this situation, but they were not very successful. At last, in the sixteenth century, there was a great revolution, the Reformation, which led to the establishment of the Protestant Church.

Members of all three classes took part in the Crusades, for these religious expeditions were, among other things, attempts to establish and maintain a perfect Christian feudal society in the Holy Land. The attempts, as we shall see, ended in failure, but in a failure which had important effects upon the way we live today.

CHAPTER TWO

The People's Crusade

WHILE THE POWERFUL LORDS OF CHRISTENDOM WERE STILL GATHERing and equipping their armies, a number of religious laymen wandered from village to village and preached the Crusade. The most successful of these preachers was a thin, bearded man, named Peter the Hermit, who rode a white donkey and spoke with fiery eloquence. He and his chief disciple, Walter the Penniless, persuaded several thousand people to follow them to the Holy Land. This is sometimes called The People's Crusade.

The expedition was ill fated from the outset. Apart from a few trained knights, the two armies were composed mostly of ignorant French and German peasants who relied on their extreme piety, or religious devotion, to overcome all obstacles. Some of these peasants were extraordinarily credulous and superstitious. One group of Germans, for example, followed a goose, claiming it had been inspired by God!

These unfortunate people had little knowledge of warfare and were badly equipped and badly led. Moreover they behaved foolishly en route, quarreling among themselves, and even attacking the Christian inhabitants of Hungary and Yugoslavia, who, naturally, fought back. Only a few thousand of them survived the long journey and reached Constantinople, capital of the Byzantine Empire, in the autumn of 1096. Emperor Alexius I (A.D. 1048-1118) had them ferried across the Bosporus to Asia Minor, placed a camp at their disposal, supplied them with food, and advised them to wait there until the main body of Crusaders arrived from Europe. They refused to take his advice, however, and set out shortly afterward to fight the Saracens. They were ambushed just a few miles from the camp and most of them, including Walter the Penniless, were killed. The survivors either returned to their homes or, like Peter the Hermit, waited in Constantinople as guests of the Emperor and joined later armies of Crusaders.

A CRUSADING ARMY

During the spring and early summer of 1097, the main armies of the First Crusade began streaming across Europe, down through the Balkan Peninsula, and into Constantinople. Historians were vague about figures in those days, but the entire "host," as it was called, probably numbered no more than two hundred thousand. In no way, however, did it resemble a modern military expedition. It was more in the nature of a migration, for at least half this number were women, children, old people, priests, monks, and other noncombatants. Many of these people had given up their homes and carried all their possessions with them. With the help of God, whom they firmly believed was on their side, they intended to take the Holy Land from the Saracens and settle there for the rest of their lives.

But let us look at a typical army, the army commanded by Godfrey of Bouillon, a hero of the First Crusade, as it marched toward Constantinople.

Godfrey's army was composed of about twelve hundred

21

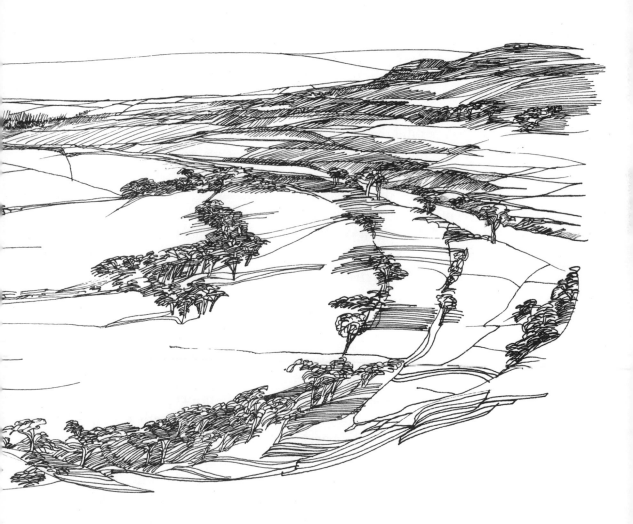

Godfrey of Bouillon's army marches toward Constantinople

knights, nine thousand foot-soldiers, including pikemen and cross-bowmen, and several thousand civilians. Godfrey and his two younger brothers rode at the head of the army with their advisers and attendants. Behind them were the knights, each at the head of his own contingent of foot-soldiers. Knights were mounted on either mules or pack animals, for their great horses were too valuable for daily use and were saved for combat. These highly trained stallions, in fact, were pampered and cared for even more than the knight's family, for without his great horse a knight would be reduced to fighting on foot like a common infantryman and would fall in the esteem of his fellow knights.

Neither did the knights wear armor as they marched, for it was heavy and uncomfortable and there was as yet no danger of meeting the enemy. It was usually carried in a baggage wagon, hanging from a wooden frame that was shaped like a cross. Armor at this time was rather primitive, not like the elaborate and beautifully engraved suits of polished metal that were worn two hundred years later. The chief item was a leather coat that was padded on the inside and had iron rings sewed on the outside. Separate pieces of leather, also covered with iron rings, were tied around the upper and lower leg and extended over the instep as well. These were called "chausses."

The knight's helmet was small and conical, with a projecting metal flap, the "nasal," to cover the nose. His shield was shaped like a kite, built of layers of toughened leather that were stretched over a frame of limewood. It was long enough to protect him from shoulder to ankle. Attached to the shield was a long leather strap that went around the knight's neck and rested across his right shoulder, so that a knight was said to "hang" his shield. This strap took most of the shield's weight off the knight's left arm, which he could then use to control his great horse, although most of these animals were so well trained that they could be controlled by knee pressure alone. If a knight was knocked off his horse in combat, he could sometimes save his life by crawling beneath his shield and staying there until he was rescued by his comrades. Besides their swords and lances, many knights were armed with battle-axes or maces, and all of them carried a type of dagger called a "scramasax."

The chief weapon of the foot-soldiers, "sergeants," was either a pike or a crossbow. The pike was simply a very long spear that was used for thrusting rather than throwing. It was primarily a defensive weapon. To protect a camp, for example, the pikemen would form a line facing the enemy, plant the butts of their pikes in the ground, and slant them forward so that the points projected at a forty-five degree angle. This bristling hedge of iron points was usually enough to stop even the most determined charge of men on horseback.

The crossbow was a bow attached to a stock so that it could be aimed and fired like a rifle, with the bow horizontal rather than vertical. One type of crossbow, "arbalest," was used to shoot darts, stones, and iron bolts as well as conventional arrows. It could be fired a greater distance and with more striking force than the regular bow, but was clumsier and had a much slower rate of fire. Eventually it was replaced by the English longbow. Besides the pike and the crossbow, the foot-soldiers were armed with daggers, and a few of them carried swords as well.

THE LEADERS

About a dozen armies as large as or larger than Godfrey's took part in the Crusade. Some of the most powerful nobles in Europe were at their head, including the son and son-in-law of William the

Conqueror, the great Norman lord who had conquered England in 1066. Only a few of these nobles, however, played important roles in the months to come. Godfrey of Bouillon was one. He became known as "The Perfect Christian Knight" in the songs and poems that were written to celebrate his actions in the Crusade. Another was Godfrey's younger brother Baldwin of Boulogne who, like many other landless knights, was determined to conquer a domain of his own from the Saracens. Then there was Count Raymond of Toulouse, a man past sixty who had already fought the Saracens in Spain and who commanded a large army of Provençals, that is, of men from the region of Provence in southern France. Lastly, there was Count Bohemond of Taranto, in some ways the most interesting of the Crusade's leaders.

Bohemond was a Norman also, a descendant of those "Norsemen," or Viking, warriors who had conquered much of Europe and for whom Normandy, in northern France, had been named. He was forty years old when he joined the Crusade, a tall, powerfully built man with shoulder-length blond hair. Bohemond's father had led an army of Norman adventurers that had conquered most of southern Italy from the Byzantine Empire. Bohemond's own lands in this region, however, were small in extent and, like Baldwin of Boulogne, he was determined to conquer a large domain from the Saracens.

CONSTANTINOPLE

All the Crusaders, from the most powerful nobles to the poorest peasants, must have been impressed when they saw the gilded domes and towers of Constantinople gleaming in the distance. At this time, and for many centuries before and afterward, the capital of the Byzantine Empire was the greatest city in the western world. No other city in Europe even approached it for grandeur, beauty, and wealth.

It was built on seven hills on the European side of the Bosporus — the narrow strait that separates Europe from Asia and leads to the Black Sea — and was protected, by a triple wall of fortifications, from the barbarians who periodically tried to conquer it. More than a million people of every known race, color, and creed lived there, and merchants came from as far away as China and India to sell their silks, spices, and other exotic wares. It had Hagia Sophia, one of the greatest churches ever built; it had the hippodrome, a vast stadium in which chariot races, circuses, and other forms of entertainment had been held since the time of the Romans; it had the fabulous Golden Gate, the main entrance to the city; it had the beautiful Galata Bridge, which spanned the arm of the Bosporus called the Golden Horn; and it had many splendid palaces and villas along the shores of the sea.

Great as it was, however, the city was not prepared to feed and shelter a horde of two hundred thousand undisciplined Europeans, especially since some of them broke into villas and robbed them, and others fought pitched battles with the Byzantine soldiers and civilians. The Crusaders behaved so badly, in fact, that Emperor Alexius ordered all but a few important nobles to remain outside the city in the camps he had placed at their disposal. As quickly as he could he supplied them with siege engines, guides, and advisers, and sent them across to Asia Minor to begin their campaign. Before they left, all the leaders of the Crusade swore allegiance to the Emperor and agreed to recognize him as overlord of any territory they might conquer from the Saracens.

View of Constantinople

A catapult

SIEGE WARFARE

The Crusaders' first conquest was of the town of Nicaea, which blocked the most important route to the Holy Land and had to be captured before they could continue. Like most large towns and cities of the time, Nicaea was built to withstand a long siege. It was surrounded on three sides by high, thick stone walls, and had the waters of a lake on the fourth side. There were wells and springs within the town, so that the attackers could not cut off the supply of drinking water. Stores of food, arrows, and other necessities could be replenished by boats coming across the lake. The Crusaders were equipped with siege engines that Emperor Alexius had given them, and with a corps of Byzantine engineers who knew how to use them.

The most common type of siege engine was simply a catapult that was used to hurl boulders against the town's wall until a hole

30

had been knocked in it or until the mortar between the stones had been loosened. When this happened, the attackers would rush forward and try to pull down a section of the wall, while other men held wicker shields, "mantelets," over their heads. These shields, however, were usually not adequate protection against the cauldrons of boiling oil, stones, and arrows that the defenders rained down upon them.

Catapults were also used to toss dead animals, balls of "Greek Fire," and other objects over the walls. Greek Fire was one of the Byzantines' favorite and most effective weapons. We are not quite sure of its ingredients, for the Byzantines kept them secret, but it was probably composed of a mixture of sulphur, naphtha, and quicklime, held together by a sticky substance — resin, perhaps — so that it would not fall apart in flight. Another sort of Greek Fire, without the resin to bind it, was shot through bronze tubes like rockets or modern flame throwers. One of these tubes was mounted on the prow of every Byzantine ship. On several occasions they were used with great success in naval battles with the Saracen fleet, burning and sinking most of the enemy vessels. The walls of Constantinople, too, were lined with these bronze tubes, and they were very effective in defending the city against barbarian invaders.

Another technique of siege warfare was "mining." The besiegers would dig a tunnel under the walls of a town, propping up the roof with wooden beams as they dug. Then they would set the beams on fire and retreat to their own positions. When the beams burned through and collapsed, a section of the wall above them very often collapsed also, and the attackers could then pour through the breach and conquer the city.

Nicaea was captured after a fairly short siege, for the Saracen commander surrendered when the Byzantine fleet sailed into the lake and cut off his supplies of food. There was much booty, as Nicaea had been the capital of an important Saracen chieftain. It was divided equally between the Crusaders and the Byzantines, and encouraged by their success, the Christians continued on their way toward the Holy Land.

DORYLAEUM

The Crusaders lived partly on food they carried with them and partly on what they were able to forage, or plunder, from enemy farms and villages along the way. So that foraging would be easier, they split into two armies — the first led by Bohemond of Taranto and the second by Raymond of Toulouse. About a hundred miles inland, near the ancient city of Dorylaeum, Bohemond's army was attacked early one morning by a large force of Saracens.

The Saracens were mounted on small, fast horses, carried curved swords called scimitars, small round shields, and used bows that had been specially designed to be fired from the backs of running horses. They wore no armor and did not carry lances.

The Crusaders were outnumbered and taken by surprise. Many of the knights, in fact, did not have time to put on their armor. They fought on foot beside the pikemen and crossbowmen, while the women, children, and other noncombatants brought up water and carried away the dead and wounded. Although they lost many men, the Crusaders managed to defend themselves until Raymond's army galloped onto the plain with banners flying and horns blaring. The two Christian armies then joined forces and drove the Saracens from the field. It was a decisive victory for the Crusaders. From then until they reached Antioch, they were not seriously bothered by the Saracens. They had other enemies, however, equally dangerous, the weather and the terrain.

32

THE LONG MARCH

Five hundred miles of hot, dry, mountainous country separated Dorylaeum from Antioch. The journey took more than four months to complete. The first part was across the Anatolian plateau, skirting the edge of the great salt marshes. The retreating Saracens poisoned many of the wells and cisterns by dropping dead animals into them, so the Crusaders suffered constantly from thirst. As they trudged along in the midsummer heat, the men sucked thorn leaves and weeds for a little moisture. Many of the animals died, and by the time the army reached the Anti-Taurus mountains in October the wagons were being pulled by sheep, goats, oxen, and even dogs.

Crossing the mountains was the most difficult part of the journey, for the autumn rains had begun and the pass, the Cilician Gate, was a narrow, muddy, slippery, and dangerous path. Entire lines of baggage animals, roped together for safety, fell into the deep ravines and gorges. Some of the Crusaders also lost their lives in this way. They did not dare to ride, but plodded along on foot, leaving a trail of discarded equipment behind them.

Many thousands of Christians died on this march, but at last the army reached the plain on the other side of the mountains and paused to rest amid the streams and orchards they found there.

BALDWIN'S CONQUESTS

While the other nobles rested, Baldwin of Boulogne set out with several hundred adventurous young knights to conquer a domain of his own. He was helped by the inhabitants of Cilicia, or Little Armenia, as this region was sometimes called. Most of them were Armenian Christians who hated their Mohammedan overlords and welcomed the Crusaders as liberators. Thousands of them flocked to Baldwin's banner during the next few months; and while

33

the main army of Crusaders continued on to Antioch, Baldwin fought and defeated the Saracens in several battles. He married the daughter of an Armenian chieftain, became Count Baldwin of Edessa (Edessa was an important town east of the Euphrates River), and gave many large fiefs to the knights who had followed him. He was the first of the landless younger sons to achieve his ambition and carve a domain from the Saracens' lands. Before very much longer, as we shall see, he was to have an even greater success.

ANTIOCH

Antioch was a commercial crossroads, one of the largest and best fortified cities along the coast. The wall surrounding it was so thick that eight men could walk abreast along its top, and was surmounted by more than four hundred towers from which the Saracens could shoot arrows and hurl rocks and boiling oil down on the enemy.

Several of the most important French nobles were so discouraged by the sight of these formidable fortifications that they gave up the Crusade and returned to Europe with their followers. They were harshly criticized by the Pope for deserting their comrades, and many of them were excommunicated, that is, denied the right to practice their religion or even to call themselves Christians. Some of these excommunicated lords redeemed themselves by joining later Crusades.

The remainder of the army, encouraged by Bohemond, Raymond, and Godfrey, settled down to besiege the city. The siege was a long one, lasting from October, 1097 to June, 1098. The Crusaders blocked all the entrances to Antioch, so that no food could be brought inside, and hoped to starve the Saracens into surrendering. The Saracens, however, were well prepared to withstand a siege, and as the months went by it was the Christians who began to suffer from hunger. They exhausted their supplies of salted meat and grain, and were forced to slaughter many of their pack animals. They had to send foraging parties far into the surrounding countryside in search of food for themselves and fodder for their precious great horses. The poorer Christians were reduced to eating cats, dogs, leather, whatever they could find, and by the end of the siege one out of every seven Crusaders had died of hunger.

Three times during this period, Saracen lords from neighboring regions led armies to rescue their brothers in Antioch, and three

The siege of Antioch

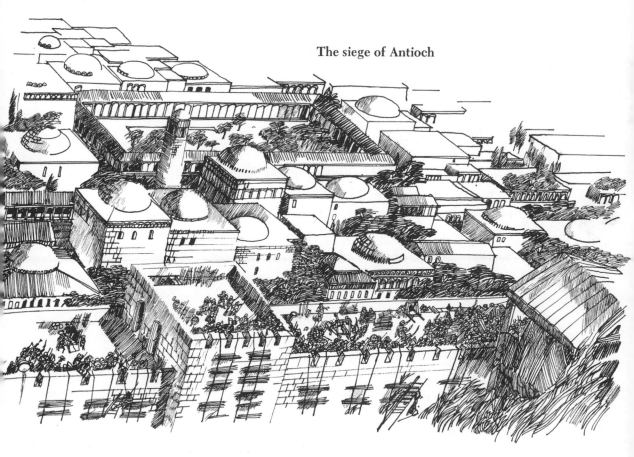

times they were defeated by the Crusaders under Bohemond's brilliant leadership. But the Saracen commander in Antioch still refused to surrender. He knew that the Crusaders were growing weaker every day, and he knew also that another large army, led by the Emir of Mosul, was coming to his rescue. Antioch, in fact, would probably not have been conquered if an Armenian captain in the Saracen garrison had not decided to betray it.

This captain's name was Firuz. He was a Christian who had converted to Mohammedanism and now wished to become a Christian once more. One night in June, 1098, he helped Bohemond and a small band of knights climb over the wall, enter the city, and open two of the gates. The rest of the Crusaders then raced into the city, carrying torches so that they could distinguish friend from foe, and within a few hours they had captured it. They behaved very cruelly, killing all the Saracens but a few who managed to escape.

The Crusaders had no time to celebrate their victory, however, for they were in turn besieged by the Saracen army under the Emir of Mosul. Their situation was desperate. They could not withstand a siege, for there was hardly any food left in Antioch and the knights were already weakened by their long months of hunger and privation; and there was no possibility of a Christian army coming to their rescue. Their only chance was to leave the city and fight the Saracens in the open. That was what they did.

Although they were heavily outnumbered, the Crusaders attacked with such fierceness and desperation that they drove the Saracens from the field and won a great victory. Bohemond took the title Prince Bohemond of Antioch and became one of the most important rulers in the East. He and his successors ruled the city and the region around it for more than two hundred and fifty years, after which time it was reconquered by the Saracens.

JERUSALEM

A full year passed before the Crusading army straggled across the sun-baked hills of the Holy Land and reached Jerusalem. Of the two hundred thousand Europeans who had set out from Constantinople two years before, only about fifteen thousand were left. Some had stayed behind in Antioch with Bohemond. Others were with Baldwin in Edessa. And more than a hundred thousand men, women, and children had died in battle, of starvation, or of various diseases including typhoid, an epidemic of which had swept through Antioch shortly after the city was captured.

Jerusalem was much smaller than Antioch, but was equally well defended. Apart from the thick stone wall surrounding the city, there was a wide ditch, a "moat," protecting it on all sides. The Crusaders knew that the city had to be taken quickly or not at all. They

The Crusaders receive supplies from Genoa

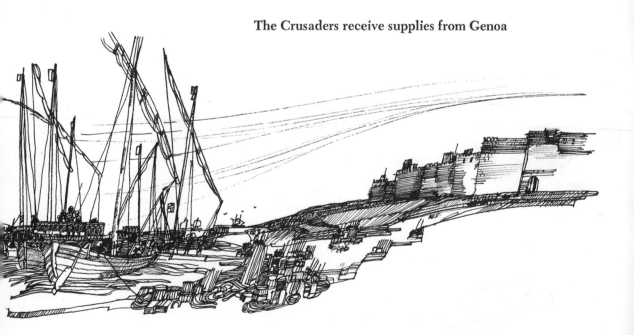

could not settle down to besiege it. They had little food; the nearest unpoisoned well was more than ten miles away; and there was no wood with which to build siege engines. The surrounding hills were covered only with brush and shrubs. The closest forest was in Sumaria, three days' march distant.

To make matters more serious still, they learned that a large Saracen army from Egypt was on its way to help the besieged city.

Then the Christians received unexpected help themselves. A fleet of ships from the Italian maritime city of Genoa dropped anchor in the harbor of Jaffa, about thirty-five miles away. They had come to help the Crusaders, and the ships carried food for both men and great horses. They also carried bolts, nails, and rope for the construction of siege engines, and a few hundred fighting men. They brought two men, the Embriaco brothers, who were famous as builders of siege engines.

Godfrey and Raymond, who were now in command of the army, sent a group of men to the forest in Sumaria. When they returned with a load of logs and cut lumber, everyone was set to work building two huge towers, each one as high as the wall around Jerusalem. The Embriaco brothers directed the work, which was done secretly, in a valley near the city. Each tower had a ladder running up the back to a platform near the top. Armed knights would station themselves on this platform, and when the tower was pushed as close to the wall as it could go, a wooden bridge would be lowered on ropes and the knights would try to cross it to the top of the wall. So that the Saracens could not set the towers on fire, green hides, that is, the untanned hides of freshly slaughtered animals, were nailed to the front and sides.

On the morning of July 13, 1099, everything was ready. While the women, children, and other noncombatants set wooden rollers

38

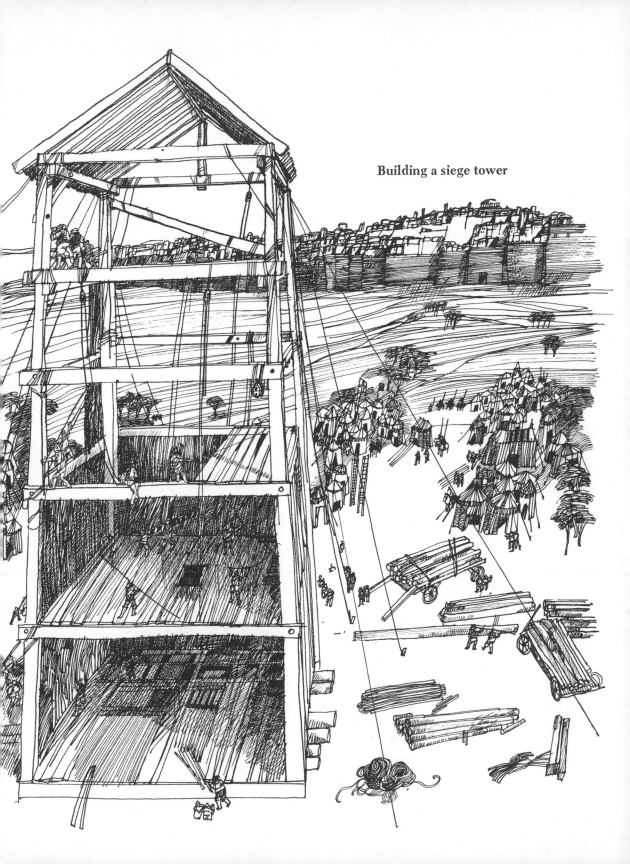

Building a siege tower

under the towers and pushed them toward the wall, several thousand men began filling sections of the moat with dirt and straw mats. The Saracens hurled rocks and other missiles down on them, but as soon as one Crusader was killed or wounded, another rushed forward to take his place.

Finally the moat was filled and then the towers pushed against the wall. Raymond and his knights encountered such fierce opposition from the Saracens that they were unable to cross the wooden bridge from their tower. But Godfrey and his men charged with flailing swords and axes and drove the Saracens along the wall. Other Crusaders climbed up the tower and joined them, and soon they had captured an entire section of the wall and were able to clamber down into the city.

Before the day ended, Jerusalem was conquered. As at Antioch, the Crusaders behaved very cruelly, slaying almost the entire Mohammedan population of the city. Then, when all resistance had ended, the nobles bathed, put on spotless white robes, and went to the Church of the Holy Sepulcher to give thanks to God for allowing them to conquer His city from the infidel.

The leading nobles elected Godfrey of Bouillon as first ruler of the Kingdom of Jerusalem. He refused to accept the title of King. It would be impious, he said, for the only true king of Jerusalem was Jesus Christ. Instead he called himself Defender of the Holy Sepulcher.

Godfrey's rule was a short one. He died of typhoid a few months later, and his brother came from Edessa and took the throne. He was not as pious as Godfrey and did not object to the title of King.

And so it happened that a landless younger son, Baldwin of Boulogne, became King Baldwin I of Jerusalem.

CHAPTER THREE

The Kingdom of Jerusalem

THE FIRST CRUSADE DID WHAT IT HAD SET OUT TO DO. IT PLANTED a Christian kingdom like an arrowhead in the heart of Islam. But it is often easier to conquer territory than it is to hold it, and from the very beginning of its short life the Kingdom of Jerusalem was under constant attack and threat of attack from its Saracen neighbors.

Baldwin ruled the little Kingdom for eighteen years and fought countless battles against the Saracens. Each battle was a crucial one, for the entire Christian army took the field. Had it been defeated there would have been no warriors left to defend the cities and the women and children. But Baldwin was never defeated. Mounted on his famous Arab stallion Gazelle, he led his army up and down the coast, conquering one town and city after another. In the meantime a steady trickle of landless young men came to the Holy Land on pilgrimage or in search of adventure.

Many of these young men joined one of the two religious-military orders that were formed during Baldwin's reign. These were the Knights Templars and the Knights Hospitalers. They served as permanent standing armies for the Kingdom, and Baldwin gave them all the help he could in order to build up their strength.

TEMPLARS AND HOSPITALERS

The Templars took their name from their first headquarters, the Temple of Solomon in Jerusalem. When a young man joined the Order, he took an oath of allegiance to the Grand Master of Jerusalem and swore to "guard the public roads, forsake worldly chivalry, and, living in chastity, obedience, and poverty according to the rule of St. Benedict, to fight with pure mind and heart for the supreme king."

A Templar's life was as closely regulated as a monk's. He ate two meals a day in absolute silence and was allowed meat only three times a week. He wore woolen clothing in the winter and linen in the summer, without ornament of any kind. His hair was cut short and his beard left rough and untrimmed. To distinguish them from the Hospitalers, who wore white crosses on black backgrounds, the Templars wore red crosses on white backgrounds. The sight of these red crosses, and the grim, bearded faces of the warriors above them, soon began to strike fear into the hearts of the Saracens. The Templars, in fact, became famed throughout both Islam and Christendom for their fighting prowess.

Like some of the monastic orders in Europe, both the Templars and the Hospitalers soon became enormously rich through gifts of land and money. The Templars became bankers and money-lenders as well as warriors, and grew so powerful that the Grand Master was treated as an equal by princes and kings. With wealth, however, came corruption, and early in the fourteenth century the Templars were accused of heresy and of practicing witchcraft. The Order was dissolved by the Pope. Some of their lands and treasures was given to the Hospitalers. The rest was confiscated by rulers of the various European countries. The last Grand Master of the

Temple, James of Molay, was
burned at the stake for heresy by
the King of France.

The Hospitalers had taken
their name from the hospital they
founded in Jerusalem to care for ill
or injured pilgrims. They fared
better than the Templars. After
the fall of the Kingdom of Jerusalem, they conquered the island of
Rhodes from the Saracens and
established an important naval
base. In the sixteenth century they
moved to the island of Malta, which they held until it was conquered by Napoleon.

Under the name "Knights of Malta," the Hospitalers still exist.
Their country is a small piece of land in the Vatican, in Rome,
Italy, that was given to them by the Pope. They are the smallest
independent state in the world; they issue passports, and exchange
diplomatic missions with twenty nations.

THE ASSASSINS

At about the same time that the Templars and Hospitalers were
being formed in the Kingdom of Jerusalem, a strange and terrifying
Mohammedan sect was organized in the mountains of northeast
Persia. They called themselves The Assassins and their headquarters
was an impregnable fortress named The Eagle's Nest.

The Assassins were an offshoot of the branch of Islam which
had ruled Jerusalem in the eleventh century and which, by mistreat-

Hospitalers castle

ing the pilgrims and desecrating the Christian shrines, had helped bring about the First Crusade. They were fanatics who believed that any Mohammedan who did not worship Allah, or God, exactly as they did was a traitor to the religion. They also believed this of any Mohammedan who did not wage a continual *jihad*, or holy war, against the Christians. Indeed, The Assassins were so fanatic that their founder, Prince Hassan ibn-al-Sabbah, killed his own son because, by drinking wine, he had broken one of the laws laid down in the Koran, or Mohammedan bible.

At the heart of the sect were the *fedais*, devoted young men who gave blind obedience to the Old Man of the Mountain, as their leader was called by the Christians. The Old Man of the Mountain soon became one of the most powerful and feared men in all Islam, for he literally held the power of life and death over the other Saracen rulers. At his command *fedais* went forth to assassinate (the word comes from the sect) those Saracen lords who had disobeyed him. *Fedais* did not care if they themselves were killed so long as they accomplished their mission, for they were convinced they would go straight to heaven when they died. It was nearly impos-

44

sible to guard against them, and they poisoned or stabbed to death hundreds of Mohammedan leaders.

The Assassins were themselves destroyed by invading Mongols in the thirteenth century, but until then they were among the most powerful enemies of the Christians. They did not attack the Kingdom of Jerusalem directly, but forced other Saracen leaders to do so by threatening them with death. In 1144 one of these Saracens besieged and conquered the city of Edessa. Although the city was not especially important, its conquest led directly to the Second Crusade, for it indicated to the Europeans that the Saracens had taken the offensive once more.

PRESTER JOHN

The leaders of the Second Crusade were the King of France and the King of Germany. Several years passed, however, before they gathered their armies and set out for the Holy Land. One of the main reasons for this delay was the widely held belief that a Christian priest-king named Prester John was leading a huge army from central Asia to destroy the Saracens. Prester John, it was believed, belonged to the Nestorian church, a Christian sect that made converts as far east as China. It was said that he had visited the Pope in 1122 and that, later, he had written a letter to the Byzantine Emperor, promising to attack the Saracens. Copies of this letter circulated throughout Europe. It began as follows:

I am Prester John, Lord of Lords by the power and virtue of God and of Jesus Christ. I am the greatest monarch under heaven and above hell. My kingdom extends over the Three Indies. Seventy-two kings are my vassals, and all the wild beasts and monstrous creatures are in my domain. There is the fountain of youth. There are pebbles which give light, restore sight, and make their possessor invisible. There are ants which dig gold and fish which give the royal purple. There is the salamander which lives in fire. When I go to war, thirteen great crosses of gold and jewels are carried before me, each one followed by ten thousand knights and a hundred thousand footmen. There are no poor in my domain, no thieves, no flatterers or misers, no dissension, no lies and no vice. Before my marvelous castle there is a marvelous mirror on a marvelous many-storied pedestal, and in this marvelous mirror I see everything that goes on in my kingdom and detect any conspiracies. I am served at table by seven kings, sixty dukes, and three-hundred-sixty-five counts. Twelve archbishops sit on my right hand and twenty bishops on my left. . . .

The letter went on for several pages in the same vein, and ended with Prester John's promise to attack and destroy the Saracens. Nowadays it would be hard to find anyone who would take such a letter seriously. It is obviously nothing more than a charming fantasy. But ignorance and superstition were so widespread in the Middle Ages that a great many people, even some of those considered well educated, *did* take it seriously. You must remember, too, that Asia was largely an unknown continent. Marco Polo had not yet made his famous voyage to the court of Kublai Khan in China, and people believed that all sorts of fantastic and wonderful things were possible there.

There is, in fact, a slight possibility that Prester John did exist. He may have been a Mongol who ruled a small kingdom in Asia. He may also have been a Nestorian Christian, since members of this sect were to be found as far east as Japan. These, however, are the only possible grains of truth in the legend. The letter was a forgery, and no one named Prester John ever visited the Pope.

DORYLAEUM AGAIN

Finally, in the spring of 1147, the armies of the Second Crusade left for the Holy Land. The German army, under King Conrad, was the first to arrive in Constantinople. It numbered about fifty thousand including women, children, and other noncombatants. The Byzantine Emperor advised Conrad not to follow the route taken by the First Crusade across the middle of what is today Turkey. The Saracens were too strong in that region, he said, and the Germans should take the coastal route, which was longer but safer, to the Holy Land. But Conrad was a vain, proud man, determined to follow in the footsteps of Godfrey, Raymond, Bohemond, and the other heroic leaders of the First Crusade, and so he set out with his army across the Anatolian plateau.

At Dorylaeum, where Count Bohemond had won his great victory, the Germans were attacked by a large force of Saracens. The Saracens had learned new tactics since the First Crusade. They did not attempt to fight the Christians at close quarters, but stayed at a distance and poured volley after volley of arrows into the ranks of the Crusaders. The knights tried several times to engage the enemy with swords and lances, but each time the Saracens fled on their small, swift mounts, and the heavily armored Germans, on their powerful but slow great horses, were unable to catch them. Then, when the knights had returned to their lines, the Saracens galloped forward again and shot more arrows at them.

These tactics were very successful. The Saracens killed or captured over three-fourths of the German army and drove the remainder back to Constantinople. There the German army joined

47

forces with the French Crusaders, who had recently arrived, and
set out once more for the Holy Land. This time, however, they took
the Byzantine Emperor's advice and followed the coastal route.

THE POULAINS

Almost fifty years had passed since the Christians had conquered the Kingdom of Jerusalem. Most of the original Crusaders
were dead, and many of their children had married local Christians
and adopted local customs. Their women, for example, often went
veiled — not for religious reasons, like the Saracen women, but to
protect their complexions from the sun and wind. They used face

48

German knights at Dorylaeum are attacked by the Saracens

powder, henna, and other cosmetics that were still unknown in Europe. Many of the men wore a loose-flowing garment called a "burnoose," which was also used by the Saracens, and ate their meals seated cross-legged on piles of carpets. They still spoke French, which had been the chief language of the First Crusade, but now it was mixed with so many Armenian and Arabic words that the French members of the Second Crusade found it difficult to understand.

The French and Germans neither liked nor trusted these *poulains* (French for colt), as they were called. They seemed more like Saracens than Christians. Indeed, there *were* a small number of

49

Saracens living in Jerusalem and the other cities of the kingdom. They were members of tribes that had signed treaties with the King of Jerusalem and were allowed to trade with the Christians and even to worship in special "mosques," or Mohammedan churches, that had been set aside for them. The Europeans could not understand this tolerance and were shocked and angered by it. To them, all Saracens were enemies and should be killed. Some of the more fanatic knights attacked these friendly Saracens in the streets and even in the mosques. The knights also fought with the *poulains* on a number of occasions, and there was much bad feeling between the two groups.

THE FAILURE OF THE SECOND CRUSADE

In July, 1148, the combined army of Europeans and *poulains* marched north and attacked the Saracen city of Damascus in Syria. The army was large and well equipped with siege engines. It was led by experienced warriors who were so confident of victory that even before the attack began they held a meeting to choose a ruler for the "conquered" city.

The commander of Damascus knew that his garrison was no match for such a powerful force, so he asked neighboring Mohammedan rulers for help. They sent thousands of reinforcements, who counterattacked and drove the Christian army away from the city's walls and into the surrounding fields and orchards. Then, instead of devoting all their efforts to fighting the Saracens, the Europeans and *poulains* began to blame each other for the defeat and to quarrel bitterly among themselves. They became completely disorganized and had no heart for further combat. Four days after they had begun the siege, the Crusaders packed up and returned to Jerusalem. The King of France and the King of Germany left for Europe with their armies shortly afterward. The *poulains* settled down in uneasy peace. The Saracens, confident now that the Christians could be beaten, prepared to attack the Kingdom of Jerusalem.

THE HORNS OF HATTIN

The various Mohammedan sects, however, also quarreled among themselves, and many years passed before they were sufficiently unified to launch this attack. The man who united and led them was Saladin, one of the greatest heroes in Mohammedan history.

Saladin's parents died while he was still a child, and he was brought up by his uncle, an important Saracen general. From the age of five or six, he accompanied his uncle on military campaigns throughout the East. He grew up, you might say, on the battlefield and learned military tactics and strategy as a boy of today learns to read and write.

Saladin was still a young man when he gained control of Egypt and the other Mohammedan countries surrounding the Kingdom of Jerusalem. He did not attack the Christians immediately, however, because he was at war with The Assassins. Finally, after the *fedais* had made several unsuccessful attempts on his life, Saladin made peace with the Old Man of the Mountain and was able to concentrate his forces against the Christians. Early in the summer of 1187, he marched with a huge army into the northern part of the Holy Land and besieged the city of Tiberias.

The ruler of Tiberias sent for help to King Guy of Jerusalem and the King gathered his entire army of *poulains*, Knights Templars, and Knights Hospitalers, and set out to rescue the city. The battle took place on a pair of adjoining hills called The Horns of Hattin. Although each army numbered about fifty thousand men, the

Saracens had several advantages. For one thing, they were led by Saladin, a brilliant general. And for another, they were well rested and well equipped. The Christians were led by King Guy, a weak ruler and a poor general, and they had marched for several days, suffering from heat and thirst, to reach the battlefield.

The Saracens attacked at dawn on July 3, 1187, and the fight raged all morning with the Christians getting the worst of it. Toward noon the remaining knights moved King Guy's red tent to the top of one of the hills and prepared for a last-ditch effort. An interesting and exciting description of this part of the battle has come down to us. It was written by Saladin's young son, Al-Afdal, who was taking part in his first military campaign.

> When the Christian King had withdrawn to the top of the hill his knights made a gallant charge and drove the Mohammedans back upon my father. I watched his dismay. He turned pale, then red, pulled at his beard and rushed forward crying, "Give the devil the lie!" So our men fell upon the enemy, who retreated back up the hill. When I saw the Christians flying, I cried out with glee, "Ah, we have routed them!" But they charged again and drove our troops back to where my father was standing. Again he urged them forward, again they drove the enemy back up the hill, again I cried out, "We have routed them!" But my father turned to me impatiently and said, "Be quiet! We have not beaten them so long as that red tent still stands." At that moment the tent was overturned. Then my father bowed low to the ground and with tears of joy gave thanks to Allah.

It was a disastrous defeat for the Christians, for their entire army had taken part in the battle and there was hardly anyone left to defend the Kingdom. Thousands of prisoners were taken. The Templars and Hospitalers were killed on the spot, for the Saracens hated and feared the members of these two orders. The other prisoners were either sold into slavery or held for ransom. King Guy himself was held captive for several months before Saladin released him.

After the battle was over, the victorious Saracens marched unopposed through the Kingdom of Jerusalem, reconquering one town and city after another. Finally, at the end of the summer, they attacked Jerusalem itself. The Holy City was defended only by old men and boys, for all the able-bodied warriors had been either killed or captured at Hattin. They fought back bravely for ten days, until the Saracens' catapults opened a breach in the wall, and then they were forced to surrender. Unlike Godfrey of Bouillon and the men of the First Crusade, Saladin and his Mohammedan warriors were merciful conquerors. No churches were desecrated, no Christians massacred, and all the women and children were allowed to go free.

It was exactly eighty-eight years since the Europeans had conquered the Holy Land and established a Christian Kingdom in the heart of Islam. All that remained of it now was the port of Tyre, in the northern part of the country, which was held by some recently arrived Crusaders.

The Crusades, however, were far from over, for other Christian knights were soon to march east and give battle to the Saracens.

Saladin and King Guy's armies at the Horns of Hattin

CHAPTER FOUR

The Third Crusade

As the fall of Edessa had brought about the Second Crusade, so the fall of Jerusalem caused the third one. Once again priests and monks traveled about Europe exhorting the people to take the Cross. Once again kings, barons, knights, and peasants gathered into armies and set out to restore the Holy Land to Christendom.

In many ways the Third Crusade was the most romantic and dramatic of these religious expeditions, for it brought into conflict two remarkable men, Saladin and King Richard Lion-Heart of England. The story of their encounter has captured men's imaginations for centuries, and many poems and novels have been written to celebrate it.

Richard Lion-Heart was thirty-three years old when he left for the Holy Land. He was a tall handsome man with broad shoulders and flaming red-gold hair, and had a reputation for being both stubborn and hot tempered. Although he ruled England for ten years, he visited the country only twice in that period, for he much preferred to live in some of the regions of France that were also part of his domain. He regarded England mainly as a source of income and often declared: "I would sell London itself, if I could find a bidder." The rest of what is France today was ruled by King Philip II, with whom Richard was often at war. When the Saracens took Jerusalem, however, the two kings declared a truce and agreed to lead the Crusade.

To raise money for the expedition, Richard declared a "Saladin Tithe." He taxed every British subject ten per cent, or a "tithe," of all his possessions. In addition, every city and town in his domain was required to supply him with horses, ships, and other equipment.

More than a century had passed since the First Crusade and it now cost a great deal more money to make war than it had then. A knight's armor, for example, no longer consisted of a simple leather suit with iron rings sewed onto it. It was made of carefully fitted plates of steel with ornate designs carved on their polished surfaces. The helmet, too, had changed in shape. It was no longer small and conical but was a large "pot" that covered the entire head and face. Underneath his armor a knight wore a "gambeson," a linen garment that prevented the metal from chafing his skin. Over the armor he wore a "grand hauberk," a loose-fitting suit of chain mail that hung from his shoulders to his knees. This equipment was very heavy and the great horses had been bred bigger and stronger to carry it. A knight in full armor had to be lifted into the saddle by his squires; and if he fell or was knocked off his mount in combat, it took two men to raise him to his feet again.

Richard's equipment was, of course, more splendid than that of an ordinary knight. It was "fit for a king." His sword had a gold-and-jewel-encrusted hilt. His spurs were of solid gold. His favorite weapon, a two-handed Danish battle-ax more than five feet long, was made of specially hardened steel and had a jeweled handle. His black Spanish stallion wore a scarlet leather saddle that was studded with gold stars and had two golden lion cubs "rampant," reared up on their hind legs, at its back corners. As a final touch of splendor, Richard wore a rose-colored silk tunic over his armor.

Discipline was more strictly enforced in Richard's army than it had been in previous Crusades. The "King's Charter," which read as follows, was nailed to the mast of every ship before it left harbor:

Richard, by the Grace of God King of England, Duke of Normandy and Aquitaine, and Count of Anjou, to all his men who are about to journey to Jerusalem by sea — health. Know that with the common counsel of approved men, we have had the following rules drawn up. Whoever on board ship shall slay another is himself to be cast into the sea lashed to the dead man. If he have slain him ashore, he is to be buried in the same way. If anyone be proved by worthy witnesses to have drawn a knife for the purpose of striking another, or to have wounded so as to draw blood, let him lose his fist. But if he strike another with his hand and draw no blood, let him be dipped three times in the sea. If anyone cast down any reproach or bad worth against another, or call down God's curse upon him, let him for every offense pay an ounce of silver. Let a convicted thief be shorn like a prize-fighter, after which let boiling pitch be poured on his head and a feather pillow be shaken over it so as to make him a laughingstock. Then let him be put ashore at the first land where the ships touch.

Richard himself traveled by ship only when it was absolutely necessary, for he suffered from sea-sickness. Thus, while the fleet carried the English Crusaders across the Mediterranean toward the island of Sicily, their first stop, Richard and a few companions went overland on horseback.

THE SIEGE OF ACRE

King Philip and the French Crusaders were the first to arrive in the Holy Land. They joined forces with the remaining *poulains*, Templars, and Hospitalers and besieged the Saracen port of Acre. Philip built two huge catapults, "The Evil Neighbor" and "God's Own Sling," with which he tried to batter down "The Accursed Tower," Acre's main point of defense. The Mohammedan garrison retaliated by building "The Evil Cousin," an equally large and powerful catapult, and bombarding the Christians with boulders and with balls of Greek Fire. The garrison was also helped by Saladin, for when the Christians besieged the city, he in turn besieged the Christian camp. This double siege dragged on for many months, with neither side strong enough to gain the victory, until Richard Lion-Heart arrived with the English.

The Crusaders now outnumbered the Saracens, and in Richard they had a general as brilliant as Saladin. Richard prevented all food, ammunition, and reinforcements from entering Acre and increased the number of attacks against The Accursed Tower. The commander of the garrison held out for several weeks, then sent a message to Saladin saying that he would have to surrender unless the Crusaders were driven away from the city. Saladin ordered his troops to attack the Christian camp, but they were thrown back with heavy losses.

"The next day," wrote an Arab historian who was serving in Saladin's army, "we saw the True Cross and the banners of the Christian kings appear on the walls of the city. An immense roar of joy rose from the Christian ranks, while we gnashed our teeth and wept with rage and humiliation. Oh, it was hateful to see the flags of the Christian kings appear one by one on the citadel and on the minaret of the Grand Mosque!"

And so the first encounter between the two great antagonists ended in victory for Richard Lion-Heart.

Richard captures Acre

ARSUF

After the conquest of Acre, King Philip returned to France with the bulk of his army. Richard was now in sole command of the Crusade. After allowing the troops to rest for a couple of weeks, he led them south along the coast toward Jerusalem. Saladin and his army kept pace inland, forcing the Christians to stay close to the shore. The Saracen archers harassed the Crusaders, killing a few men and a number of great horses, and finally, on a plain near the village of Arsuf, there was a pitched battle between the two armies.

Richard placed his pikemen and archers in the front rank, with the mounted knights behind them. The flanks of the Christian line, the most vital sections, were defended by men who had most experience fighting the Saracens: the Knights Templars on the right flank and the Knights Hospitalers on the left. Richard and the other Crusaders were in the center.

The Saracens attacked at midmorning and we have a wonderful description of the battle. It was written by a monk named Ambroise, who was in Richard's retinue.

First came the trumpeters and drummers, sounding their instruments and yelling so loudly that God himself would not have been heard. Then they moved away and wave after wave of Negro and Bedouin infantry raced forward, shooting their arrows and letting fly with their lances. They threw the first line of our infantry into disorder but made no impression upon the men of iron behind them. Then the Saracen cavalry, their axes and sabres flashing in the sunlight, charged the Knights Hospitalers, hoping to turn our left flank, and you could see nothing in the turmoil of dust, shrieking horses and shouting men. . . .

The Hospitalers held firm, though they suffered great losses, and the Grand Master of the Order rode up to Richard and begged permission to attack. His men, he said, would have to give way unless they could take the offensive.

Richard told him to be patient, that the Christians would attack as soon as the main body of the Saracen army was closer. But at that moment one of the Hospitalers broke ranks and galloped headlong toward the Saracen lines. His charge was infectious, and soon the entire line of knights was in motion. Ambroise wrote:

The Hospitalers charged in good order, and were followed by Count Henry of Champagne and his brave companions, and Count James of Avesnes and his followers. Count Robert of Dreux and the Bishop of Beauvais charged together. From the left, by the sea, charged the Count of Leicester with all his men, and there were no cowards among them. Then all the army was charging — the Angevins, the Poitevins, the Bretons, the Manceaux, the Normans, the English, and all the other divisions. Oh, the brave knights! They attacked the Saracens with such vigor that each one found his man, planted his lance in his entrails, and hurled him from the stirrups. . . . When King Richard saw that the charge had begun without waiting for his command, he clapped his heels into his horse's flanks and launched himself at full speed against the enemy. And such was his prowess on that September day before Arsuf that all around him I saw the bodies of Saracens with their bearded heads planted like cabbages in the field.

The magnificent charge broke the Saracen line and they abandoned the field to the Christians. And so the second encounter between Richard Lion-Heart and Saladin ended in victory for the Crusading King.

JERUSALEM AND JAFFA

Arsuf, however, was not as important a victory for the Crusaders as Hattin had been for the Saracens. After Hattin the Kingdom of Jerusalem lay open and undefended to Saladin's victorious troops. After Arsuf the Saracen-held cities, including Jerusalem, were still strongly defended, and Saladin's army, though weakened by losses, remained intact.

Saladin decided not to risk another pitched battle with the "men of iron" from the West. Instead he employed scorched-earth tactics, moving down the coast ahead of the Crusaders and razing every town and village, burning all the crops, and driving the livestock across the border into Egypt.

Richard spent several months rebuilding Jaffa and another port, so that he would have strong bases on the coast, and then led his army over the hills toward Jerusalem. On Christmas Day, 1191, the Crusaders saw the white houses of the Holy City gleaming in the distance, but that was as close as they got to them, for Richard reluctantly decided to return to Jaffa. The Mohammedan garrison in Jerusalem was too strong and well supplied, and Saladin's army hovered nearby, ready to pounce upon the Christians if they besieged the city. Besides, the winter rains had ruined a large part of the Crusaders' stores of salted meat and grain.

After his return to Jaffa, Richard opened truce talks with Saladin, trying to gain permission for Christian pilgrims to visit the shrines in Jerusalem. But the English King was not as good at negotiating as he was at fighting, and as month after month went by with no progress, he grew impatient to return home. He was suffering from a disease which was probably caused by lack of fresh fruit and vegetables in the Crusaders' diet; his treasury was nearly empty; and he had learned that his younger brother John, whom he had left in charge of England, was plotting to take over the country and have himself crowned king.

After one more unsuccessful attempt to besiege Jerusalem, Richard went to Acre and prepared to depart for Europe. He had no sooner reached the port, however, when a messenger galloped up with news that Saladin had attacked Jaffa. Although he was anxious to leave for home, Richard took part of his army and sailed back down the coast to rescue the city.

He got there in the nick of time, for a priest swam out to the ship and told him that the Saracens had captured part of Jaffa and were battling for the rest of it. Without bothering to put on armor, Richard grabbed his Danish battle-ax, leaped over the side, and waded ashore. His men followed him, and after a fierce battle they recaptured the city and drove the Saracens into the hills.

The next morning Saladin and Richard reopened truce talks, and at last they reached an agreement. The Christians could keep a strip of land ninety miles long and ten miles wide, running along the coast between Acre and Jaffa. This would be the Kingdom of Jerusalem. Also, they would be allowed to go on pilgrimage to the holy places in Jerusalem and other Saracen-held towns and cities. In return, Saracen ships would be allowed to use the ports of Acre and Jaffa, and Saracen merchants would be allowed to trade with the Christians.

And so, though he did not reconquer the Holy City, Richard's Crusade could be called successful, for once again there was a Kingdom of Jerusalem.

CHAPTER FIVE

The Fourth Crusade

RICHARD LION-HEART DIED IN 1199, SIX YEARS AFTER HIS RETURN from the Holy Land. As befitted a great warrior, he died in battle, killed by a stray arrow as he was leading an attack against one of King Philip's French castles.

Later in the same year the Pope proclaimed another Crusade, and once again a number of important nobles took the Cross. The Crusading spirit, however, had grown weaker and most of the new Crusaders were hard, ambitious men, more interested in acquiring booty than in restoring Jerusalem to Christendom. They decided to attack Egypt, the center of Saracen power, and asked the "Doge," or ruler, of Venice to build a fleet of ships to carry their armies across the sea.

The Doge, an extraordinary man named Enrico Dandolo, agreed to build the fleet in return for 85,000 silver marks. He knew that the nobles had impoverished themselves to arm and equip their armies, that they would never be able to raise so much money, and that, when they failed to do so, he would gain control of the Crusade.

This happened exactly as he had foreseen. The nobles were

able to raise only a small part of the 85,000 marks, and Dandolo refused to give them the fleet unless they agreed to help him conquer the city of Zara, on the coast of what is today Yugoslavia. Some of the nobles angrily refused, for Zara was a Christian city. But most of them agreed, and so the Doge of Venice turned the Fourth Crusade into the Crusade Against Christians.

Zara was no match for the Crusading army and fell after a short siege. After looting the city and killing most of its inhabitants, the Crusaders once more made plans to attack Egypt. But once again Dandolo changed their minds. By pretending that he wanted to restore the rightful ruler to the throne and also by promising enormous amounts of booty, he persuaded them to attack Constantinople, the capital of the Byzantine Empire!

Although he was ninety-five years old and totally blind, Dandolo personally directed the attack and succeeded in conquering the great city for the first time in its history. The Crusaders behaved very cruelly after the conquest, treating the Byzantines exactly as they had the Saracens. They burned down a large part of the beautiful city, killed many of the inhabitants, and carried away shiploads of gold, silver, and jewels, as well as statues, paintings, tapestries, and other valuable works of art. The Byzantine Emperor was forced to flee, and a European noble was set upon the throne in his place. The Europeans ruled Constantinople for sixty years, when it was reconquered by the Byzantines. During that entire period there was constant warfare between the two groups of Christians. This allowed the Saracens to build up their strength and helped bring about the ultimate downfall of the Kingdom of Jerusalem.

THE CHILDREN'S CRUSADE

Many Europeans disapproved of the Fourth Crusade. It was

shameful, they said, for Christian to fight Christian while Saracens still ruled Jerusalem. The Pope himself was angry with the Crusaders and excommunicated many of them; but then he relented and allowed them to practice their religion once more.

Few men took the Cross during the next few years, for the kings and nobles were too busy fighting among themselves. But early in the spring of 1212 a young shepherd boy named Stephen of Cloyes appeared in Paris and began to preach the strangest Crusade of them all.

We know little about Stephen except that he was an orphan whose parents had died in an epidemic when he was five years old. There were thousands of these unfortunate children in Europe during the Middle Ages. A few of the luckier ones were cared for by monasteries or foundling hospitals. A few others, like Stephen, were allowed to work as shepherds or farmhands in exchange for clothing, shelter, and a simple diet of goat's milk, cheese, and coarse bread. But most of these orphans had to look out for themselves as best they could. They wandered in bands about the countryside, begging or stealing food, sleeping in the fields, and dying by the hundreds of hunger and disease.

Stephen was rather tall for his age, very thin, with brilliant blue eyes and an unkempt mat of brown hair. He was barefoot and dressed in rags when he arrived in Paris, and must have looked very much like any other street urchin. But there was something different about him, for he was a fiery and eloquent preacher and people soon began to come from miles around to hear him speak.

Stephen said that God had come to him in a vision and had commanded him to lead a Crusade of children to the Holy Land. Where adults had failed, he said, children would succeed, for their minds and hearts were pure and uncorrupted. They would not even have to fight the Saracens, but would persuade them to give up Jerusalem without a struggle.

To the superstitious and ignorant people of the thirteenth century, this did not seem strange or unlikely, and they responded enthusiastically to Stephen's preaching. Thousands of children took the Cross, and many adults helped by donating food, clothing, and even a few horses for Stephen and his chief disciples to ride.

In June, 1212, an army of nearly twenty thousand children began marching south toward the port of Marseilles on the Mediterranean coast of France. At their head, in a gaily decorated cart, rode Saint Stephen of Cloyes, as he was now called. He wore splendid clothing, which had been given to him by wealthy admirers, and was accompanied by an escort of noble boys and girls on horseback.

The children carried little food and water, for they depended on the charity of the peasants whose lands they crossed. But it was a hot, dry summer, a summer of drought and famine, and the peasants had little to spare. Within a few days many of the younger children, some of whom were only five or six years old, began to fall by the wayside, unable to go on. Others fell ill or died in the weeks that followed. By the time the Crusade reached Marseilles there were only about seven thousand children left.

Stephen had told his followers that God would cause the Mediterranean to part for him as He had caused the Red Sea to part for Moses and that they would then walk across on dry land. When this failed to happen, several hundred of the children accused Stephen of being a false prophet and abandoned the Crusade. The others, however, still had faith in him, so they settled down in a camp outside the city and waited for a miracle to solve their problem.

The following week Stephen received a visit from two mer-

chants named Hugh the Iron and
William the Pig. They offered,
as an act of charity, to supply
enough ships to carry the children to the Holy Land. This
seemed to be the miracle the
Crusaders had been waiting for,
and they accepted joyfully. A
few days later, accompanied by
crowds of well-wishers, they
trooped down to the waterfront,
boarded the ships, and set sail.

For eighteen years nothing
more was heard of them. They
did not arrive in the Holy Land,
so everyone believed they had
been lost at sea. Then, in 1230,

The children's crusade

a priest named John the Unlucky came to Marseilles from Egypt
and told the citizens a horrifying story. He said that he had been
one of several young priests who had accompanied the Crusade.
Three days after leaving Marseilles, a great storm had sunk two of
the ships, and all the children aboard them, including Stephen of
Cloyes, had drowned. The rest of the flleet had gone on to the
Saracen port of Bougie in North Africa! There the children had
been taken ashore and sold into slavery. This had been arranged by
Hugh the Iron and William the Pig, the priest said. With his own
eyes he had seen the leather sacks of gold coins they had received
as payment from the Saracens.

The people of Marseilles were very angry when they heard the
priest's story, for many of their own children had taken part in the

Crusade. They set out to find the two evil merchants and punish them for their treachery. They were too late, however, for Hugh the Iron and William the Pig had been hanged a few years earlier as punishment for other crimes.

As far as we know, John the Unlucky was the only member of the Children's Crusade to return to France. The others probably spent the rest of their lives as slaves of the Saracens.

THE GERMAN CHILDREN

The tragic French expedition was only part of the Children's Crusade. While Stephen and his followers were still on their way to Marseilles, a twelve-year-old German boy named Nicolas of Cologne began to preach the same Crusade. Nicolas came from a family of well-to-do farmers and was encouraged by his father, a proud, vain man who boasted of the miraculous deeds his son Nicolas the Prophet would perform in the Holy Land.

Nicolas and the children at Hamelin

Like Stephen, Nicolas was an eloquent preacher and he soon had many thousands of followers from the towns and villages of north-central Germany. In one of these towns, Hamelin, he was so successful that nearly all the children took the Cross and left with him. This became the basis for the legend of the Pied Piper of Hamelin, who first charmed the rats away from the town, and then, when the citizens refused to pay him for performing this service, charmed the children away with sweet music from his flute and never brought them back.

Late in the summer of 1212, two armies of about fifteen thousand children each set out for the coast of Italy. The first army, led by Nicolas, crossed the mountains of western Switzerland. It was a much harder journey than the French children had made, and only about one-third of the army reached the port of Genoa, on the Mediterranean coast. The others either fell ill and died, turned back, or were fortunate enough to be taken in by peasant families along the way.

Nicolas had also promised his followers that God would cause the sea to divide so that they could cross it on dry land. When this did not happen, a few hundred children accused him of betraying them and abandoned the Crusade. Some of these children were adopted by Genoese families and later became important merchants. The rest of the army followed Nicolas down the coast from port to port, where they tried either to make the sea divide or to find ships that would carry them to the Holy Land. A couple of dozen were taken aboard ships in Pisa and transported to Acre, but the others were unsuccessful and continued walking south until they reached Rome, where they saw the Pope.

"The very children put us to shame," the Pope wrote afterwards. "While we sleep, they go forth gladly to conquer the Holy

Land." He praised the children for their courage and religious devotion, but discouraged them from continuing the Crusade. They were too young, he said, and should return to their homes until they had grown up. Then they could take the Cross and go forth to fight the Saracens.

The children disbanded, and most of them, including Nicolas, vanished into the surrounding countryside. Nothing is known of their fate.

The second army of fifteen thousand children fared even worse. They left Germany at the beginning of autumn and, while crossing the Swiss Alps, were caught in a snowstorm in which several hundred of them froze to death. The survivors reached the coast of Italy and wandered south in Nicolas's footsteps, gradually diminishing in number until they too had been swallowed up in the Italian countryside.

Of all the children who had left Germany, only a handful reached the Holy Land and only a handful returned to their homes. And so this strange, sad Crusade, which tells us so much about the way people thought in the Middle Ages, accomplished nothing but the deaths of thousands of children.

CHAPTER SIX

The Fifth Crusade

INSPIRED BY THE CHILDREN'S EXAMPLE, THE POPE PROCLAIMED YET another Crusade in 1215. This one was jointly commanded by a Spanish cardinal named Pelagius and by King John of Jerusalem, and, like the Fourth Crusade, it set out to attack the Saracens in Egypt. If the enemy could be driven out of Egypt, the Crusaders reasoned, then they would be forced to surrender Jerusalem and the rest of their territory in the Holy Land as well.

The Crusaders' first objective was Damietta, an important city at the mouth of the Nile river. The siege lasted over a year, with many attacks and counterattacks, and for a while it seemed that neither side would gain the victory. Perhaps the most interesting thing that happened during this time was that Saint Francis of Assisi visited the Saracens. Saint Francis tried to convert the Saracen ruler to Christianity, but though the Saracen — a wise, tolerant man named al-Kamil, who was Saladin's nephew — allowed Saint Francis to preach and to enter and leave the Saracen camp without harm, he remained unconvinced of the superiority of Christianity to Mohammedanism. Saint Francis returned to Italy without having succeeded in his mission. Soon after his departure an epidemic of

73

St. Francis preaches to al-Kamil

bubonic plague struck the area. Though the Christians lost many thousands of men, the Saracens lost even more. In fact almost the entire population of Damietta was wiped out by this dreaded disease, and the Crusaders had merely to enter and occupy the deserted city.

Al-Kamil offered to exchange Jerusalem for Damietta, provided also that the Crusaders agreed to leave Egypt. King John and his leading nobles were eager to accept this offer, but Cardinal Pelagius refused. The Cardinal was a proud, fanatic man who considered it ignoble to negotiate with the enemy. It was also said, perhaps truthfully, that he wanted to conquer all of Egypt and become famous so that he would be elected Pope when the present one, who was past ninety, died.

The Crusaders split into two factions, those who supported King John and those who supported Pelagius. There was such bitterness between the two groups that on several occasions they fought with each other in the streets of Damietta. Finally, however, Pelagius had his way and the army set out to attack the Egyptian fortress of Mansura, on the road to Cairo.

This proved to be a disastrous mistake, for al-Kamil had sent for reinforcements and inflicted a severe defeat on the Crusaders. The result was that the Christians not only lost thousands of men in the battle, but they were forced to abandon Damietta as well.

Needless to say, Pelagius did not achieve his ambition of being elected Pope. In fact he was severely reprimanded by the Church for having refused al-Kamil's offer.

THE SIXTH CRUSADE AND THE POETS' CRUSADE

The Holy City was briefly restored to Christendom by Emperor Frederick II of Germany a few years later. The Emperor's Crusade was really only a peaceful visit to the Holy Land, for he did not fight the Saracens. Instead he won by treaty what other Crusades had failed to win by force of arms. He signed a ten-year agreement with al-Kamil that gave the Christians all of Jerusalem except the two chief Mohammedan mosques. Al-Kamil was willing to sign such an agreement because he was at war with other Saracen leaders and did not have enough troops to be able to fight the Christians at the same time.

The Saracens, however, did not keep their end of the bargain. Soon after Frederick had returned to Europe with his army, and there was no longer any danger of his attacking them, they reclaimed the Holy City. This led to the short, tragic Poets' Crusade.

The leaders of this ill-fated expedition were Count Philip of

Nanteuil and Count Thibaut of Champagne, Norman lords who were also well-known *trouvères*, or poets. Unfortunately, they were better poets than they were generals, for they were badly defeated by the Saracens shortly after they arrived in the Holy Land. Philip of Nanteuil was taken prisoner, along with over six hundred of his men, and thrown into a dungeon in Cairo. While waiting for Thibaut to pay his ransom, he composed a number of poems, one of which sums up very nicely the unfortunate Crusade.

Ah, France, douce contrée,	Ah, France, sweet land,
Maudite soit la journée	Cursed be the day
Où tant de vaillant chevaliers	That so many brave knights
Sont devenus prisonniers!	Were taken prisoner!

**Philip of Nanteuil
in a Cairo dungeon**

SAINT LOUIS' CRUSADES

King Louis IX of France, who was later canonized as Saint Louis by the Church, led two Crusades against the Saracens. The first one, called the Seventh Crusade by historians, took place in 1249, when the thirty-year-old monarch sailed to Egypt with an army of more than sixty thousand French nobles and their vassals.

The Crusade began successfully, for Damietta fell after a short siege. Al-Kamil, now a very old man, once again offered to exchange Jerusalem for the captured city, and once again the Christians refused. Like Cardinal Pelagius, King Louis considered it ignoble and unchristian to negotiate with the enemy.

Several months later, following in the footsteps of the Fifth Crusade, the army set out to attack Mansura. Al-Kamil died while the attack was in progress and his son became ruler of Egypt. The defense of Mansura, however, was conducted by a group of former slaves called Mamelukes. Their leader was a cruel, utterly ruthless man named Baibars the Crossbowman.

Although he was cruel and ruthless, Baibars was also a brilliant general. Under his command, the Saracens inflicted a crushing defeat on the Crusaders. King Louis was taken prisoner and held until an enormous ransom (the equivalent today of more than a million dollars) had been paid. Most of the Crusaders were either killed in the battle or died of hunger and disease, and many years passed before France recovered from the loss of manpower.

After his release from captivity, King Louis spent some time in the Holy Land, strengthening the little Kingdom's defenses. On two occasions the Saracens invited him to visit the Christian shrines in Jerusalem, but each time he refused. Although he wanted nothing more than to make such a pilgrimage, he would not enter the Holy City until he had conquered it by force of arms.

Twenty years later, in 1270, Louis led another Crusade, the Eighth, this time against the Saracen city of Tunis in North Africa. There was no fighting, however, for the Crusaders were struck by epidemics of typhoid, typhus, and dysentery soon after they landed. Thousands of them sickened and died, including King Louis. The King's last words were: "Jerusalem! Ah, Jerusalem!" After his death, the Crusaders abandoned the siege and returned to France.

THE END OF THE KINGDOM OF JERUSALEM

Baibars the Crossbowman assassinated al-Kamil's son and gained control of Egypt. Determined once and for all to wipe out the Kingdom of Jerusalem, he declared a *jihad* and swept across the border into the Holy Land at the head of a huge army.

Town after town swiftly fell before him, and the alarmed Europeans launched two Crusades in an effort to stop his progress. Both of them failed, for the Christians were unable to cooperate

The death of King Louis

with one another. While the *poulains* quarreled with the Crusaders and the Templars quarreled with the Hospitalers, Baibars the Crossbowman destroyed their castles, conquered their towns and villages, and sold their captured women and children into slavery.

Baibars died shortly after he had conquered Antioch, but the *jihad* was continued by his successor, another savage Mameluke. Finally, in 1291, the last Christian stronghold, Acre, was conquered. After its conquest, the Saracens razed the city to the ground so that the Christians could never again land troops there. Thus, nearly two hundred years after the First Crusade had established a Christian kingdom in the heart of Islam, nothing remained of it but a few scattered fortresses that were soon abandoned. By the end of the century, the crescent banner of Islam waved from one end of the country to the other.

For the next two hundred years Christendom was on the defensive, struggling to prevent the Saracens from overrunning Eastern Europe. The high point of the Saracen advance was reached in 1453, when they conquered Constantinople from the Byzantines. After that, although they gained some territory in the Balkans, the borders between Christian and Mohammedan nations did not change very much.

There were a number of so-called Crusades during this period. They were really only military expeditions, however, for they lacked the religious fervor of earlier Crusades. Europeans had grown skeptical of the whole idea of Crusades and only the very pious responded to the Pope's appeal for an expedition to restore the Holy Land to Christendom, or to reconquer Constantinople from the Saracens. They were skeptical because several Popes had declared Crusades against Christian kings with whom they had quarreled! The last Pope to proclaim a Crusade against the Saracens, Pius II in

1464, was forced to abandon the idea when only a handful of nobles responded.

RESULTS OF THE CRUSADES

At first glance it might seem that the Crusades were wholly destructive, that they accomplished nothing but the deaths of hundreds of thousands of people and created a lasting heritage of bitterness and distrust between Christians and Mohammedans. But this is only partly true. The Crusades were indeed as destructive as most wars, but they had positive results as well.

Their chief benefit was the exchange of ideas and cultures that they brought about between East and West. The Saracens, for example, passed along their invention of algebra and their discoveries in astronomy and medicine. They also transmitted a priceless store of Greek art and literature which they had preserved from destruction. This helped bring about the Renaissance, for it was these great works of art and history and literature, hitherto considered lost, that gave impetus to the humanist revival that swept across Europe, beginning in the fourteenth century.

And on another level, the Crusaders returned to their homes with sugar, maize, lemons, melons, cotton, muslin, glass mirrors, and many other things that had been previously unknown in Europe.

Perhaps the most lasting benefit of these religious wars, however, is the word crusade, itself, and the image it creates. In reality the crusades had various motives, not all of them good, but today the word "crusader" brings to mind a brave man setting forth to give battle for an ideal. He no longer carries a sword or wears armor or rides a great horse, but the best of the crusader's spirit lingers on, and we may be thankful that there are still men willing to sacrifice everything in an unending crusade for a cause in which they believe.

Index

81

Index

RICHARD SUSKIND was born in New York City and attended public schools there. In 1943, he joined the Army and served in the 8th Armored Division as a machine gunner in the Battle of the Bulge, in Holland and in Germany. After the war he continued his education on the G.I. Bill in such schools as Columbia University, the University of Florence, the University of Paris, the Juilliard School of Music, and the Conservatory of Music in Paris.

In 1948, Mr. Suskind served with the Israeli Army during the war for independence. He then joined the merchant marine, and in the next two years traveled around the world twice. He has lived all over the world, including two years in Italy, five in Paris, and for seven years on the Spanish island of Ibiza, part of the Balearic group in the Mediterranean.

Mr. Suskind has been writing since the age of fifteen and is the author of three books and more than one-hundred articles and short stories. He is married and has one son.